Engelboc

Robert DiNapoli

ENGELBOC
Robert DiNapoli

Published by Littlefox Press
PO Box 816
Kyneton VIC 3144

ISBN 978-0-6480838-3-2

Cover artwork by Jon DiNapoli

as ever,
for

Caz, Jon, Mim and Bec

Thanks and Acknowledgements

grateful thanks to my closest and canniest readers,
Carolyn Masel, Christine Mathieu and Jill Morrow

and to my friends and acquaintances who've taken time,
each in their own way, with my poems and other writings and offered
welcome encouragement and counsel, prominent among them

Denise Brown, Kate Burridge, Anne Colwell, Amanda Dyett,
Annaliese Griffiss, James Keegan, Katie Mirabella,
Deborah Phelps, Sue Rechter, Richard Wrigley

I acknowledge with equally deep gratitude the support of everyone
who's helped to make my efforts in The Melbourne Literature Seminars
such a delight, with a special shout-out to the regulars of
the MLS Refectory Series.

My friends at *Arena Magazine*, especially my editors Alison Caddick,
Sarah Bailey and Valerie Krips, have been unstintingly kind to me
and my work. You're all legends.

Christine Mathieu and her small press, Littlefox, have made this book
possible, with editorial panache, splendid company and much practical
know-how. All poets should be so well looked after!

'The Look-Out Man (It's All in Yer 'Ead)' and 'Stars'
have appeared previously in *Arena Magazine*.

Other poems of mine, along with a number of essays,
both published and unpublished, can be found at

http://themelbourneliteratureseminars.com.au/category/news-and-articles/

bob.dinapoli@yahoo.com.au

Tell all the Truth but tell it slant—
Success in Circuit lies
Too bright for our infirm Delight
The Truth's superb surprise

As Lightning to the Children eased
With explanation kind
The Truth must dazzle gradually
Or every man be blind—

                    Emily Dickinson

Contents

Introduction

This is not *quite* a book about angels, who, if they exist, can be neither seen nor addressed directly by most of us moderns. Perhaps, like the faerie of more recent antiquity, they once stood plainly visible to our forebears, but such beings have since withdrawn peripherally, lensed to the margins of our consciousness by our present-day habits of thought. Yet we have always been instinctive pattern seekers, and angels have, historically, made many different kinds of patterns: theological, aesthetic, cognitive, psychological. You don't have to be a literal believer to take them up and consider them. This, for me, constitutes a half-way house between the naïveté of literal belief and scepticism's cold, objective eye. To meddle meaningfully with angels demands both great naïveté and a knowing scepticism . . . at the same time.

The poems in this collection, which range from the personal and concrete to the speculative and abstract, trace hints of the angelic in many quarters. You might have to squint to see anything angelic at all in some of them, but it's there. None are *about* angels as such, but angels are about them, in all sorts of odd ways, often glimpsed in passing, from oblique, corner-of-the-eye angles. As messengers, angels pass between otherwise incommensurate orders of being. They can be brash and annunciatory, or so subtle you don't know they're there. The tidings they bear can be glad or awful. Like the voices you might hear in a silent room or the play of breezes on a grassy meadow, they can haunt with the possibility of presences sensed but not quite realised.

They've been represented across ancient literatures in many guises, from the 'feathered souls' of *The Epic of Gilgamesh* to their walk-on parts in the Old and New Testaments, reprised with modern twists in works by writers such as William Blake, Franz Kafka and Thomas Mann. In every historical period of Western art, they have been painted and sculpted too many times to name. They have played modern cinematic roles from Clarence the angel in *It's A Wonderful Life* to the sober grey docents of *Wings of Desire*.

This collection's title, *Engelboc*, is my own Old English coinage which means *Angel Book*. It is simply descriptive but uses tenth-century words, from a time when angels could be entertained in thought without any violent suspension of disbelief. The Anglo-Saxon poets who used words such as *engel* and *boc* inhabited a liminal age which retained many

1

of the ancient world's certainties about the coexistence of spirit and matter, while anticipating their separation, which led eventually to our modernity's submission to the latter and deep uncertainty about the former. In these poems, I toy with the *idea* of angels as a kind of thought experiment, to allow my modern imagination to contemplate their presence and activity as a play of subjunctive meaning: as hypotheticals, contra-factuals or 'invisibles' (as I call them in 'From the Galleries'), they allow me to address possibilities too easily discounted in the thought of our age.

Fruitfully? Profitably? Read on and judge for yourself.

Focal Length: the Magi

Of course. How else could it have ever begun?
That distance. Hands engaged beneath the eyes.
The mother's gaze upon her suckling child.
The artisan's appraisal of her work
as it takes shape, just there, beneath her chisel.
The weaver and the goldsmith, blacksmith's sledge,
all work at just that critical focal length,

from which, as if our fingers were the roots,
and our nerves the stem that blossoms in the brain,
the world pushes back upon our consciousness.
Our works work us, each licks the other's shape
into some semblance of a finished thing.

A mutual regard that's taken on
inflections almost daily curiouser:
technologies metastasise apace,
and 'hand-held device' now means an implement
of subtlety and power to shift the world
around our heads. Already I can see
so many necks that bend, on train or bus,
stalks supporting faces that incline
above the new-born babe, new magi bathed
in the ether of its birth, unheralded
by angels' song or humble shepherds' awe.

From the Galleries

J.M. Barrie's play Peter Pan: or, the Boy Who Wouldn't Grow Up *contains a famous scene in which the failing fairy Tinkerbell is saved by the belief of all the children in the audience.*

Young William Blake saw angels in the trees
of eighteenth-century London, of all places.
A few of those he later spoke to proved
distinctly heterodox in their opinions.
Which goes to show you simply never can tell.

I've sat by friends whose pens moved with a will,
once they had stilled their minds to overhear
what passed beneath the looping chatter within:
mice behind the skirting boards, or specks
that drift within the aqueous humours of thought,
unseen until we gaze upon blank walls.

'Invisibles' I've come to call them since:
agencies I only half believe
invest the billowing folds of space and time,
like notes from somewhere else that someone left
slid silently among your folded linen,
slipping out while you're busy changing sheets.

But half a belief is better than none and may,
in fact, prove best when turned to catch the light
just *so*—refracting possibilities
and holding off the modern mind's galumph
toward some childish certainty of fact.
Just let them *be*. They know what they're about.
Like clever eighteenth-century domestics
they leave the room before the guests arrive,
their only signature the table laid
exquisitely for others to enjoy.

They've had their portraits taken, now and then:
the feathered souls of the dead in *Gilgamesh*.
The lions of Assyria with wings

4

and burly haunches planted on the earth.
The seraphim who kneel across the ark
to guard the jealous mystery of God.
Renaissance masters, deft at feathered grafts
on human shoulder blades.
                                    Always wings:
those paddles of the sky that signify
an aerial nature. Ariel, lion of God
and English pun—though Puck is just as nimble—
and even Tinkerbell, whose fading light
draws sustenance from children's fierce belief.

Thus we mask them, with carnival *visages*
sketched and etched by our imaginings.
But *who* in heaven's name are they, for real?
Behind such semblances lie only more:
a pattern of tree-bark hinting at a face;
cloudscapes, waving grass, that fleetingly
propose a ship, or footprints, glimpsed and gone.
The black dog that emerges from the night
as if a clot of shadow sprouted legs.
Sunlight that glints off water onto wall,
casting flickers we mistake for life
and talk to plaster like Moses to his bush.

Just hinted faces? Just voices that ascend
from silence when the world lies fast asleep?
Angelos is Greek for 'messenger'—
but, if we overhear, whose speech? from where?
Cosmic eavesdrops (no return address)?
Intercepts with no Enigma key?
Or *billets-doux* in heaven's treasure hunt,
left for us to find that tease and taunt
as we peruse the winding galleries
which thread the haunted houses of our thoughts,
where every other word comes whispered soft
from somewhere behind our misdirected backs.

Behind the Lines

Sir Francis Bacon, Sir Isaac Newton and John Locke are often cited together by William Blake as the tutelary spirits of renaissance and enlightenment rationalism, reductive science and empirical philosophy. In Blake's poems they appear as a kind of unholy trinity whose influence helped to confine the human imagination beneath a de facto *assumption that material phenomena and processes alone offered valid testimony in the courts of reason.*

All who hear love's distant clarion
will understand at once they've been dispatched
as secret agents: patient of all woes
that time and space inflict upon desire
but hearing too a higher melody
that answers their distress and solitude—
a message shone from tiered authorities
whose balconies curve over this cold pit
whence witnesses look down and play their parts
to move the players who stir the sand below.

Bacon, Newton and Locke have bound us here,
who built with clinkers from creation's fire—
mainly walls and fences, architraves
of fact set high on piles of evidence
that prove our earth-clenched downward tendency
our only truth, forbidding all demur.
Reason's courts they've rigged to serve their turn
as their constabulary—muscle, heat—
enforcing *a priori* quarantines.

While we whose second thoughts still give us pause
avert our eyes, walk quietly on streets
that thrum with couriers who pelt along
on horizontal errands, shifting stuff
and bearing messages for earthly bars
that long ago stopped answering the call
from any power greater than their own.

But we have heard, and struggle still to hear,
that still small voice amidst cacophonies
of behemoth mechanism set to churn

6

reality to pixelated dust.
The glow we cup so tenderly in thought
cannot be scanned. Beneath our eyes and hands
strange wonders dance; the desiccated bones
and dust of ages slowly taking shape
as living form restored to love and flight.

Crossing the Line

Above my house the stars you cannot see,
bundled by the horizon out of sight:
Centaurus, Crux, Canopus, Carina.

And I recall the stars the heavens wore
when, as a child, I learned their names and ways:
Polaris, Cygnus, Cassiopeia, the Bears.

My change of state below is writ above.
Unseen the hands that weave my errant path,
obscure the mind enamelling my fate.

Timor Mortis Conturbat Me (**Not**)

'The fear of death distresses me', the refrain from a poem by William Dunbar sometimes called 'The Lament for the Makers'. The parenthetical 'not' is my own bravado.

The government today announced its plans
to exfoliate the city's transport weave
for planned completion by 2030.
The date stuck in my mind. I did the maths.
Seventy three I'd be, if all plans held,
when I could ride an as-yet unbuilt train
through what I hope for now is empty space
and not some row of homes to be demolished.

My own bypasses, stitched four years ago,
might last the distance to that happy day.
They might, but then again . . . and then I found
a moment's readjustment of perspective
left me quite easy with that lottery.
For nearly all my life I've gathered reeds
plucked here and there from other thinkers' pools
and woven baskets, metaphysical weirs,
quite useless as containers of the soul,
but pretty in themselves and fit at least
to sit upon my shelves and gather dust.

Señor Minotaur

In 2015, I was obliged to undergo coronary bypass surgery. My cardiologist warned me that the procedure can have curious psychological ramifications. I was not disappointed . . .

Splayed upon the step-stoned pyramid,
I hold my sutured heart up to the sun,
integuments obsidian-unlaced.
Coronal fire lights coronary art,
my arteries' new labyrinth exposed,
the roof of Daedalus flung back to bare
the stately home of Señor Minotaur,
whose options had been narrowing all the while
he blundered and bashed against the winding walls
and rubble silted up the corridors.

The lances of the picadors spit blind rage—
born in Taurus, I should have seen this coming.
But centred in the flood of theatre-light,
I still can make this offering of myself
to all the powers that flay and slay and stay,
unpack my inmost throbs to suit my soul
with better-tailored Saville-Row panache.

Entanglement

Quantum? Karmic? Does it signify?
Either way you've entered a domain
forbidden you by reason's protocols:
no action at a distance, agencies
that form a pinhead kick-line just to mock
all solemn arbiters of fact and truth.
'One smile and suddenly nobody else will do'.

Hearts enmesh, across long spans of years,
across the chasm into which the dead
drop out of sight, and out of whose same night
are born the living. Mere coincidence?
Where's your great-great-grandma? Where were *you*
when Leonardo drew Vitruvian Man?

You see where this is heading? What if death
were just a skinny-dip in Lethe's stream?

What makes one heart completely lose its place
in space and time when another heart draws near,
just one of millions otherwise passed by
without a shiver, without the merest flick?
Could such a wind arise without a cause?
Could it come down to unschooled appetite,
stoked by mere phenomenal stimuli?

Get back into your Skinner box, my friend.
I'm having *none* of that! Hearts collide,
like asteroids and planets 'round their sun.
Sometimes the impact's glancing, just a kiss.
Another will strike a marriage of true minds.
Perhaps but rarely, hearts might intersect
yet fail to hold. From each a little piece
gets carried away beneath the other's skin,
unrecognized perhaps, a stowaway,
and, borne off without ceremony, lost,
it pines on distant shores and tincts the mood

11

of its host, who scarcely understands its throb.

Could such entanglements, if they extend
beyond the boundaries of space and time
as we perceive them between waking and sleep,
still tug, still register an otherwise
invisible affinity wrung deep
beneath the wind-whipped currents of our thought?
How could we tell? Mere speculation fails
to satisfy all of reason's border-guards
and has to be detained for questioning.
At least until some final morning stills
all thought, all doubt, all stern interrogation,
and peals love's liberty at heaven's gates.

With the Dust of the Stars in Her Eyes

Ancient near-Eastern tradition speaks of a personified wisdom who acts as a kind of midwife to God's creation of the cosmos. Her role is both aesthetic and formative: she dances to inspire the creator's primordial act and informs its issue with her power to pattern and direct. In later traditions she is given the Greek name Sophia.

And who am I to speak of love to you,
my lady Wisdom, Sophia of the stars,
who danced before the countenance of God,
soliciting all-making words from his lips?

Am I to beg you dance a step with me,
on my arm to cross the tessellated floor
as ranks of heavenly courtiers applaud
my boldness and your ladyship's good will
that stoops to grant an honest heart's request
from one who sees no other eyes but yours
and in them every yearning of his heart?

Out on the moonlit colonnade shall we
resort to sit and speak of all that moves
the world beneath the floor of our pavane
in murmured notes of true philosophy?

The Tessellated Floor

The heavens lie beneath the dancing feet
in chambered gold and lapis lazuli,
the zodiac set true with lustrous art
where courtiers process from house to house,
exchanging mask of fish for bull or lion,
metamorphic choreography
that rings its changes on the earth below.

Above, the serried ranks of higher being,
their wings outspread and faces raised to see
the true-still centre of their whirling gyres
that, turning, manifest the moveless heights:
the axle-tree of all our restless being,
the spindle that transects each circle's round,
the mast that heaves each morning-sail aloft.

Innocence and Open Eyes

The classical idea of a lost 'golden age' is marked by the profound irony that it was a time when gold still lay buried in the ground and had not yet been dug up to vex human behaviour with greed and its attendant violence. When it was, the human world experienced a 'fall' comparable to Adam and Eve's. A lesson for capitalists everywhere . . .

And the eyes of them both were opened, & they knew that they were naked.
      Genesis 3:7

So cold, the blush of shame, whatever heat
might prickle beneath. The bottom fallen out
of situation, market or your drawers.
Facing the cheeky winds with both yours bared.
Embarrassment of riches, gold hauled forth
from decent subterranean sequestration,
earth's secret mischief: Ovid's Age of Gold
made so by the total absence of the stuff,
its revelation purchased far too dear,
the price-tag tucked away or else misread
till carried to the front of the checkout queue.
Too late then, under all those watching eyes,
to walk your rash selection back to the shelves.

We thus persist along mistaken paths,
too mortified to retrace any steps.
Yet is that angel standing by the gate
thick bouncer or an usher? Its sword of fire
a 'keep out' sign or torch to light our way
to tables booked for us many lives ago?

No way to tell, but on our trudge through time,
we stumble now and then on scenic views:
chance encounters (or so they seem to us)
with other souls, or with the works they've left,
that flush our eyes of local clod and weed.
Love's beacon flares and all is made anew,
that unrelenting boof at Eden's door
now waving welcome in arcing sheets of flame.
Our nakedness exchanged for robes of state . . .

. . . till we awake, clutching our rags of need
'round weary limbs which we must stir once more
to the longer road of error's wandering way.
Yet buoyed, our mental theatre still lit
with scenes and sensibilities that outpace
all tedium of heavy, sucking mud
and distance rolled out ever farther ahead.

Until at last we learn to flip the view,
reverse the perspective, and come at length to know
those revelations for the waking truth
and all the rest a slog through murky dream,
from which, in time, we school ourselves to wake.

Gnostic Variations: the Diplomatic Pouch

Gnosticism was an ancient philosophical tradition, condemned by the church as heretical, which insisted that the proper sphere of the human was wholly spiritual, and that we came to be mired in the physical world by a kind of cosmic detour we should never have taken. Our task now is to recover a clear sense of our loss that, with the support of beneficent spirits, will help us reclaim our lost patrimony.

Come to yourself upon an alien shore,
behind you your but half-remembered home.
Yourself, but in a space you can't make out,
your head still vague, aswim in vain regrets.
Thrown or set down? Exile or emissary?

Angels have made this run time out of mind:
habitués of courtly eminence
they nonetheless set forth on errands known
to them alone and their dispatching heights.

Downward, outward—wings make damned good sense—
they negotiate the incommensurate deep,
identities intact and eyes aflame,
to limitary worlds of time and edge,
where they perform the will they've carried here
like papers in a diplomatic pouch.

While, we, mere wanderers, cannot conceive
such focus: sharp, precise, exquisitely shaped
like the alabaster fireplace-surrounds
that cup the blazes of heaven. In the dust
we improvise our campfires out of scrap
that once was Adam, in the flagging hope
that somewhere out there someone might discern
our smoke by day, our wavering flame by night.

Herald Angels

As messengers and heralds, the news angels deliver can be very good (the euangelion *announced by the angels at Christ's nativity) or a bit more confronting (the trumpets of doom sounded to herald the apocalypse). Either way, when angels do speak, the world responds. The human mind commonly finds itself lost for words at such junctures. The fallen angels whose image closes this poem have their own agenda . . .*

They will not sing for that last falling night,
as once they sang to usher in first dawn
and in the stable mid-point of all time.
On that night asses spoke and oxen hymned:
brute nature answered with a human voice.

But today our voices gargle in our throats,
our tongues rolled up and bundled for the night,
the *logos* stuffed behind glottal doors to grunt;
the feeling intellect, right reason, soul,
dismissed as phantoms, and in their places stones
hacked crudely to the look of ox and ass,
braying and roaring, jeering at the fools
who threw away their birth-right on this mess.

While behind us, angels of calamity
descend to serve our notice of eviction.
Another bad-news booting down the stairs
of being's long gradation. Summer-school,
remedial necessity's sharp switch
across our backs, beneath the heel of time.
Long sentence no remission countermands:
no show-piece calling forth of Lazarus,
no gleam to pierce the depths of our defile.

Lie still and pray the spinning planets' reel
might, in some fullness we cannot foresee,
unweave these cerements that swaddle us
like baby-corpses dangled on the skein
of threads extruded from the spinnerets
of our arachnid minders, angels crisped
and snugged into creation's empty pockets.

Kakangeloi: the Age of Lead

for Donald Trump

*There's angels and there's angels. Here and in 'The Division Bell', I've employed the word
kakangeloi (literally 'bad angels' or 'evil messengers') to name those traditionally identified as 'fallen'.
Let's say their company does not conduce to flight.*

Substance settles, sinks its mass and weight
through insubstantial effluvia and mist.
Kick it, son; that's gravity, that is,
what's dense, compacted, able to impose.
Let weaker wills but *bear*. What must be *borne*,
now *that's* the stuff we want to traffic in—
possess our share of it, appropriate
its heft, its presence, its authority
so we can wear it like a knuckle-duster,
get down to business, get things done.

Don't mind those shadows hovering in the air.
That was us once, airy-fairy flits.
We've since learned better. *They* call it a fall—
I say we've just come to, down here, and now
we've work to do. This place needs sorting out.

Mearcstapan

An Old English word that means 'border-stalker' or 'haunter of the marches'. Broceliande is a mysterious march-land in Arthurian legend, taken up by the twentieth-century poet Charles Williams as a realm of incipient forms (some would say dreams), which haunt its depths, waiting on their chance to manifest in our world as living beings. To wander there is to risk losing touch with the 'real' world in your mind. The episode of the fairy-king Pluto's abduction of Herodis (Eurydice), the wife of Orfeo (Orpheus), occurs in a Middle English poem titled Orfeo. *Unlike the classical myth, it has a happy ending.*

The borders are, of course, where monsters be,
lie twisted at the margins of the maps,
distended nostrils venting reek and spray.
Marsh and march, indefinite hinterland,
water clogged with dirt and dry land swamped.
The dark beyond the door that stands ajar,
waving off the night it can't exclude,
while we sit by the fire, keeping watch.

Grendel. Heathcliff (his very name an edge).
The fairy king who snatches Orfeo's queen
from behind the wall of shields encircling her.
The Green Man lurking in the foliage,
between the branch and what unfurls the leaf.
Each bigger than life, each bursting at the seams
with raw vitality, not summoned yet
to answer the command of reason's forms,
to serve, like angels laddering the skies,
the will that cut the cloth of Jacob's dream.
They sway upon the wind from Broceliande
and stir amidst the boughs of trees that stand
along the boundaries, waving supple limbs,
discharging living shapes both fair and foul.

The human venture has coasted this frontier
down all the stretch it's nosed through time and space.
Here and there and elsewhere. Waking. Dream.
The borderlands and crossroads where two ways
inflect each other, receive and send the shades
that haunt such thresholds, where the mason's trowel
that points creation's mortar tocks its bricks

20

one against the other on their bed
of yielding matter that answers to design,
until time's wind breathes stone into its bones.

But now the living powers pass us by
while we stand rooted in our fixity,
helpless to cope with what comes over the bourn—
all spirits spooks, all living thought a terror
of possibility we can't command.
We legislate, conscript philosophy
as doorman for our increasingly seedy dive
to guard the threshold, turn away what comes
inappropriately clad to suit our whim,
our will tricked out in constabulary chic:
principles august and absolute,
smart truncheons cocked to deliver our final say.

And thus we stand on our contested march,
unsure which way to face—what's in? what's out?
Opinions vary, good will's begun to fray
past all our stabs at stitching it up again.
Wisdom's fled and left her door ajar
like idiocy's slack jaw and dangling tongue.
Our strand proves just a sand-bar as we watch
the waters creep, behind us and before.
Canute at least knew they would not retreat
at his command, ironically adduced
to show his earls the limits of his sway.

And what awaits? Some crossing? Some transgression?
Some corner we will round with no idea
of what exactly we will then confront?
Drink up. The barkeep's rung the closing bell,
and, far out in the eastern desert, day
is just about to grab the sky and light
whatever world we've summoned from the deep.

Night in the House of Play

Virgil served as Dante's guide through his Inferno *and* Purgatorio. *One of the elder poet's refrains is 'look again'. The cursory glance too often overlooks the spiritual underlay of what it regards.*

Hidden passageways that flank the halls
whose carpets pad the hush. Eyes that shine
from portraits hung on walls in gilded frames
that divert the gaze of any who might *see*.
Voices that tip-toe, indistinguishable
from winds betrayed outside by tell-tale leaves.
Do not test the shadows with your sight.
And do not press the silence to your ear.

Try the looking-glass and don't forget
to turn what it reflects the other way.
'Look again', as Virgil said to his charge,
not *at* but *around*. The secrets show themselves
circumstantially to those who *play*,
who understand the stark necessity
of indirection's rule: see one, see two—
the echo's hint, the corner of the eye,
harmonics lingering half-heard on the air.

Puckish: Taking It in

They may want simply to remain unseen.
They may appear no more than stippled light.
The tree outside my window's tipped with fire
as autumn kindles mind's reflective cool.
A sun set in my brain long years ago
(when certain youthful passions crashed and burned)
that only now begins to show its light
around the bitter horizontal edge
I'd always thought was just a dead straight line,
but proves in fact a spheroid planet's curve.
We live too close to wonder that wears masks
on scales our infant souls can scarce conceive.
It takes some time to swallow a cosmos whole.
Babies' open mouths *ung* everything:
beach balls, chairs, or curtains drawn across
the window that displays the world they'll see
aswarm with presence their elders disallow—
the airy hosts we rude mechanicals
bustle past unseeing as we tend
to the business of the globe, having forgot
that an honest 'O' is our only fit salute.

La Vita Nuova: Cartography

In some ways, we serve as angels to one another. Our every significant relationship or encounter delivers a message from a previously unknown world. Like the tongues of angels, such messages can take a lifetime's unpacking, laced with comedy, tragedy and a fair whack of slapstick. La Vita Nuova is the title of Dante's account of how his fortuitous encounter with Beatrice Portinari on a piazza in Florence upended his life forever.

Why our orbits crossed still puzzles me.
From far away she came, in keeping with
my sense of distance in that long ago.
How much turned upon those spindly seconds!
Fates enwoven past all reckoning:
from astral heights she stooped below to me.

Perturbation? You don't know the half of it,
Sir Isaac! Fate's banana peel let drop
like courtly lady's silk remembrancer
or bratty whoopie cushion placed just *so*.

Her face alone I saw, feet in the air,
as I wondered when or whether I'd hit the ground.
Once she left, once stayed, her avatars
of different aspect, stunning different me's.
Portentous comet, its flight upending all,
and nestled moon of love that sails my nights.
Yet both calamitous, shifting hill and wave,
tearing up old maps and drafting new
as though the world had moulted its own skin.

A Trip to the Fair

. . . but nobody was there.

Renaissance, 'Trip to the Fair', lyrics by Betty Thatcher, from *Scheherazade and Other Stories* (1975)

One day we thought to cheer ourselves at a fair.
With gold we crossed the palm that spun the wheel
and sat ourselves behind the lowered bar.
Gears turned and raised our gondola aloft.
The ground fell below, but almost all at once
the shudders, stops and starts set the chairs asway.
The earth rocked like a leaf caught on a breeze.
We could not read our bodies' shrill alarm
and feared a fall; our hands could grasp no stay
but the length of iron that held us in our seat.
Backward we reared and rose toward the crown;
the world grew small between our useless feet.
Descending we beseeched to be set free
before that fateful wheel could spin again.
The palm obliged, satisfied with our gold,
and we debouched as field and fold drew near.
Startled by the spectre of our fear,
we stumbled to the exit, doomed from there
to separate paths, fortune's exiles banned
to widely sundered quarters of the wind.

Sendings

At the root of all story, Telemachus sets forth
to seek out signs of Odysseus' return.
Hope deferred since ever he could think,
new breath expands his chest, Athena's sending,
logos whispering all will be well:

the one whose absence drew a grieving veil
across the heavens' splendour now draws near.
The seam of sea and sky begins to fray,
admitting glory none had dared to hope
would ever again touch headland, face and heart
with light not glimpsed for twenty years and more.

While in the royal house at Ithaca,
his mother's suitors wallow thoughtlessly,
consume his stores so prudently laid by
and sneer at any thought of royal rebuke.
Yet overhead, before her loom withdrawn,
she weaves their fates with cold and dextrous hands.

Something Rays through

Sometimes, if you're very lucky, poetry itself can do the angels' job for them.

I sing for fun beneath the sun
and not for some fee or renown.
Of the songs I sing some few take wing,
the rest hardly worth but a frown

of curdled ambition that sought recognition
for mastery, genius and craft,
as if such could come from out of the scrum
of desire and envy and graft.

No. To speak what is true, something rays through,
a beam from some distance or height.
My poetry's lines are just slat-shuttered blinds
adjusted to let in the light.

Stars

In 1993 my wife would laugh
when I arose, a stepladder deity,
in one hand star-charts, the other flourishing
gummed phosphorescent paper circles and stars,
to spangle our newborn's ceiling with the skies
of cloudless northern nights. It worked so well.

Ten years on, war's shadow leans aloft;
we're selling up and moving hemispheres
to live where different stars will shape the night
above our heads. The room must have fresh paint,
so while the radio delivers word
of massing troops and fey diplomacy,
I once again ascend the ladder's stair
with scraping tool and bucket to remove
the heavens I had spread, a different god,
of aspect terribly transformed—the stars
fall at my approach like winter snow,
while our children's laughter fills the rooms below.

The Angel Wakes

The seasons' ebb and flow have stranded me,
sent from another world, beneath these stars.
On alien streets the faces pass me, closed
on shuttered thoughts that swerve invisibly.
Did someone send me? Where should I turn *my* face?
I pat my sides in absentminded search
for my credentials. Behind me I can hear
the shirr of wings; I turn to look but see
just air, whose diamond clarity disturbs
some memory lodged deep within my mind.

The Barrow Down

Loves learned and re-learned, for so long yearned,
on paths mistaken, long rows forsaken—
their furrows skewed and only trued,
through turning years and falling tears,
by back-breaking toil over stubborn soil,
thus setting straight what only too late
you saw as error, a mortal terror
that you sowed under, a fatal blunder
amidst good seed, a griping need
that's stunted the best and eaten the rest,
to your despair.
          Your gasps stir the air
of futile regret, desire not met
with answering smile, a barren defile
as bare of bloom as windswept tomb,
a barrow-down beneath whose frown
you stop and gaze through gathering haze
at the slot that descends through the bank that bends
above your hair as your feet grope the stair
that conveys your worth beneath the earth
to be assayed midst treasures arrayed
by long-dead hands now swathed in bands
against the wall of the earthen hall.

Your bed lies long and the sleep is strong
that fastens your eyes and swallows your sighs.
Neither hope nor despair nor comfort nor care
attends your repose while morning's rose
blossoms aloof above barrow-roof,
times without number the while you slumber
long ages away past thought of day,
a silent seed not to be freed
beneath a long night of auroral light
that sets a crown upon the mound.

Till day returns and sunrise burns
in eastern sky as, from on high,

one descends from the uttermost ends
of mind and space, sent to unlace
the swaddling bands from your infant hands
and the barrow unroof to daylight's proof
that kisses your eyes with dawning surmise
of joy re-arisen, your long earthen prison
a retreating dream whose vapours stream
back down the wells of your mind, whence their swells
first rose in power to blight and sour
the very day in whose light you now play.

The Division Bell

Kakangeloi in many guises stalk
the porticoes of power, while their kin,
the better sort, still toil their best to mend
the mayhem wrought by their rambunctious sibs,
attend us secretly and do not wish
to trumpet their part in the scenes we now behold.
Yet the time draws near for all to show their hands.
The division bell will ring and all must up
and declare our yeas or nays for once and all.
Consider this a handy voter's guide,
for the issues blur, the choices we must make
grow tangled in these latter days when wolves
parade their sheepskins torn from carcasses,
that, flayed, stuff trenches, covered with loose earth,
where morning glories writhe and branch and gleam,
fluorescent underneath the lowering cloud.

But for all the rot, for all the gutting loss,
the real business happens somewhere else.

The mists make visible the solar orb,
otherwise outshone by its corona.
Its veil lays bare a widow's muted face,
a beauty whispered, drawn into itself.
Thus darkness cannot wholly stash its prey
beneath the hem of its cloak. Fugitive gleams
betray its larcenies, venal and grand.
We play our part, to wait and holler 'thief!'
at every splinter of light that slits the gloom.
Like shepherds answering their dogs' alarm,
invisibles, when they hear us, will attend.

The Exiled Duke and the Angelic Doctor

The fictional Prospero of Shakespeare's The Tempest *(the exiled Duke of Milan) and the historical John Dee (Elizabeth I's court astrologer and occultist) are both embodiments of the renaissance magus, a compound philosopher/enchanter thought to communicate with angelic intelligences.*

The Exiled Duke

'Milan'. A good iamb, otherwise a null:
the iamb no *I am*. Milan no more,
then who have I become upon this isle?
A castaway, discarded by my own
and, truth to tell, not all that much put out
by anonymity and solitude.
I have my books, of family such scraps
as fate has left to me. Then there's my art,
that captivates my earth and air recruits.
Long to learn, but really not much chop
once mastered, simple jugglery of shows.
My brother's conned my part across the sea,
so now I have to shape some role to play
for spirits, monsters, crabs and baby girl.

The Angelic Doctor

Within my glass I scry to see who stands
beyond the doors, behind the curtains hid.
An angled-mirror, round-the-corner peep
past where unaided eyes can find their way.
Names, distinctions, choreography
of what the busy world takes for a play
of whimsy, unaware that *it's* the joke.
This chorus line of shining face and wing
has rung the ages with their voices raised
beneath the vaulted joinery of heaven
for longer than earth's rolled upon its plate:
a pea to keep a fair princess awake,
a bangle for her off-day court attire.

33

The Lookout Man (It's All in Yer 'Ead)

A hemispherical parable inspired by Iain McGilchrist's The Emperor and His Emissary, *an extraordinary psycho-literary account of the bicameral brain.*

Lefty schemed the heist: he'd read the plans
of tunnels, tripwires, sensor cells and vaults.
The heavy gold shone dully in his eyes.
Righty had to watch for all his mate
could not foresee: the unexpected guard,
dozily dutiful, making another check;
the extra stair that might precipitate
a ruinous fall; the constabulary swoop;
the informer who'd commanded total trust.
For all these things sharp Lefty had no eye.
Righty did his bit by taking them in
and trying to foresee a thousand more
impediments and checks that might befall.
Righty had to use imagination,
which Lefty always had to keep at bay
if he'd have any hope of mastery.

Righty was Lefty's best friend, though he did not
reciprocate the honour, solely bent
upon articulating all his plot.
Oh, he could talk, could Lefty: words came quick,
obedient to his will. "We'll take it easy,
lolling by the pool, for all our days."
But all he saw on that lounger was himself.
Righty was taciturn—he had to *think*,
assembling all the pieces of the puzzles
set by time and chance, or, at the least,
the ones that he could grasp. Lefty, his friend,
he had no doubt, would see him right in the end.

A flawless ensemble, together they advanced
toward their gleaming goal; that stashed in bags,
they then unwove the turnings of that maze
and made for open air. "Sorry, mate,"
said Lefty over his gun, "you done your bit."

34

Righty never heard the loud report.
Head down, full tilt, divested of his friend's
capacity to see what didn't suit,
he never heard the sirens' keening wail
nor ever saw the strobing blues and reds,
before the handcuffs manacled his wrists
and the law struck with its truncheons at his knees.

Cyberia

cp. Shoshanna Zuboff's The Age of Surveillance Capitalism

As the new night deepens, souls sit still at screens,
and algorithms chitter in the dusk.
Bot and malware sizing up each click,
crystal-balling mysteries of will:
desire anatomised, search-items float
in analytic formaldehyde to yield
the secrets of a compromised desire.

As rhetorics inflame, the world-mind cools.
Idiotic tweet-slings clot the air
till no one's thoughts can breathe, and hidden wills
look on to calculate where profit lies.

The word that lit the world so long ago
now sliced and diced in texting acronyms
(MAGA, POTUS, WTF, LOL)
and truncated politburo portmanteau
(libtard, fucktard, cuckservative, soyboy).
All haste, all unreflective, reflex jerks
no more aware than a jellyfish's flinch.
Blake's polypus, a gelid digestive tract
fixed on seabed, deaf and blind and dumb,
stands forth now in the glaring light of day,
or at least the raddled blue-end glow of screens.

Look away! Take book in hand and read.
Scrawl on paper, ancient art not slaved
to prying eyes and ad-men's pop-up lurks.
They don't see us. They circle in our minds
like sharks that herd the school into a ball
that they may feed the more conveniently,
like sheep set forth to graze on pasturage
with teeth too sharp and steely to be real . . .

Spider-Bait

The data-engineers assure us now
we're nothing but the aggregated clicks
of our online personae: netted, bunched
in poseys that reveal, to the scrying eyes
of information-science boffinry,
our once and future tendencies. We lie
like chickens plucked and dressed for baking trays,
our mental coastlines mapped, our chambers scoured
of all they hold that isn't bolted down,
like temple vessels borne to Babylon
to grace the feasts of those whose interests lie
in mere aggrandisement of heaped-up stuff.

They count on us to walk into their snares
all unawares, like flies that can't work out
what's gummed their wings until the eight-legged dusk
begins to fall. By then it's much too late.
Our only hope's to leave the beaten track
and mess with their actuarial aplomb.
They want our traffic? Screw that for a joke.
Play up and show some spontaneity.
If we conform we lose. Just stick it out
and wag it in their faces. They'll survive.
Don't buy what they're selling. It's just a bill of goods
that nobody needs. Get used to solitude.
The Facebook ship of fools will drag you down.
Get off that gangway and learn to live again.
Social credit's just more spider glue.

Morning Song

for C.M.

Because she curls beneath the bedding
like a cat,
her *rrmphs* both mews of comfort
and protest,
even though she bid me wake her now,
last night while in possession of all
her faculties.

Her consciousness will dawn at last
as out-thrust foot—
its toes as ripe for tickling as a babe's
and telling as if gifted with five tongues
just what they're asking for.

I reach for the peppermint moisturizing cream . . .

Le Chevalier de la Cote Male Taylé

In Book IX of Malory's Le Morte D'Arthur, *Brewnor arrives in Arthur's court wearing ill-fitting and bedraggled armour. He is ridiculed by Kay with the mock title 'The Knight of the Ill-Cut Coat'.*

The world declines to shift to suit my will,
nor can I trim my heart to fit its pinch,
and so, ill-sorted, are we forced to go,
an awkward three-leg race where stumbles reign
and lookers-on are in it for the mock.
So Kay mocked Brewnor, and so my fate mocks me,
but kindly, now I've served my tale of years,
whose tally holds much sally and sortie,
whence I've returned bedraggled, drubbed and scotched.

But no morning yet has found me slug-a-bed,
for every time I hear the faerie horns
I spurn good counsel and gallop out the gate,
into a world whose shape I've never conned,
whose ways are thick beset with clutching roots
that hurl my mounts and me to thumping checks,
in clanking heaps of man and horse and steel.

The hardest part is rising from my back
to find again my feet and swimming head,
while voices titter from the shrubbery.
My surcoat, as you see, has borne the worst
of all my misadventures yet preserves
some vestige of my blazoned heraldry.
So call me *Cote Male Taylé*, if you will.
Such honesty as I possess must own
a name that suits my dishevelled state so well.

The Featherless Fall
or, the Flying Mango

for Caz, with mango chutney

sum sceal on holte   of hean beame
fiþerleas feallan—   bið on flihte seþeah,
laceð on lyfte,   oþþæt lengre ne bið
westem wudubeames;   þonne he on wyrtruman
sigeð sworcenferð,   sawle bireafod,
fealleþ on foldan,   feorð biþ on siþe;

(*The Fortunes of Men*, ll. 21-26)

In the woods, down from the towering tree,
featherless, one will fall. Nonetheless
that one will fly, flutter through the air,
a fallen fruit from the branch. Among the roots,
his wits darkened, his spirit stripped away,
he plunges to earth, descends—his life departs.

The facts lie plain for everyone to see,
though critics have contended high and low.
This creature—human?—tumbling through the air
sans wings, as if he'd rushed into the rain,
his umbrella leaning desolate in its stand,
forgotten in his hurry down the hall.
Now gravity unpacks the weight of 'fast',
as though he'll not return to tell the tale.
His glide-path vertical: 'Earth to man—
you're on the beam for touchdown, running hot.
Can you kill your speed?' No time to squawk.
Below, X marks the spot where he will splat.

But he can fly for now, a falling fruit.
The mango-man careens the space-time chute
toward the root-bed whose entanglements
will sieve his splattered vitals, sculpt his pith
anew amidst the topmost boughs, whence he,
like Ferris wheel or pater-noster lift,
will drop and drop again, until those wings

take root between his shoulders, clutch the air,
and rise from endless play of up and down
parabola to hyperbolic bow
that slings its shafts toward unfathomed heights.

Postscript: Coyote Song

A small tribute to Chuck Jones' sequence of Road Runner cartoons, which served as a kind of scripture for my childhood. Angels can be tricksters (and tricksters angels) as well. You have been warned . . .

Thus the psychodrama, but is that all?
Simple enough to conjure up such spooks,
the black and white, with wand-like pencil flourish.
But in between, *entr'acte*, as it were,
what giggles from what souls hid in the wings?
Will some ironic coda round the show,
mopping up that dread and all that blood,
sprayed liberally across the properties?
What chance those scenes might not have been real at all
but served some other purpose altogether?

Perhaps some figure, his evening dress austere
yet frayed at knee and shiny in the seat,
might step before the deep black velvet cloth,
all spangled with comets, stars and galaxies,
and, smiling with lopsided authority,
tell us the truth of what we'd just beheld.
Expositor and comic exegete,
he sidles up to his insinuation
of how completely wrong we'd got the play,
made earnest of the game and game of that
from which our souls' immortal fates depend,
leaving us suspended in mid-air
like Wile E. Coyote looking down,
the brink he'd just raced off too far behind,
the ground between his feet too far below,
time only for his placard scrawled with *YIKES!*
before he plummets to the earth once more,
once more to take up residence and the chase.

CPSIA information can be obtained
at www.ICGtesting.com
Printed in the USA
BVHW041529070619
550466BV00004B/4/P